ILLUMINATE THE RUINS

Copyright © 2018 Sarah Bethe Nelson

All rights reserved. This book or any portion thereof may not be reproduced or used in any manner whatsoever without the express written permission of the author except for the use of brief quotations in a book review.

Cover photo © 2018 Justin D. Frahm
Design by Justin D. Frahm
This book was set in Iowan Old Style.

ISBN: 978-0-692-17757-0

First Edition 2018
10 9 8 7 6 5 4 3 2 1

ILLUMINATE THE RUINS

Sarah Bethe Nelson

CONTENTS

Wildfire	1
True Spring	2
Day	4
Rainbow Trout	6
A Complicated System	7
Portuguese Sweet Bread	8
How The Devil Does	9
Ready Or Not	10
Signs Say Love, Love More	11
Half Mine	12
Wading The Shallows	14
The World Awakes	15
The Universal Word Is *huh*	16
Evening	18
Night Creatures	19
Blind Games	20
Perfect Geometry	21
Sex & Love Anonymous	23
I Change Only The Names Of The Living	25
False Spring	26
Hymn	27
Memories Meet Memories	29
Pastels	30
Bright Ribbons	31
Two	32
Location	34
Brothers	35
Me, Not A Mother	37
Sonogram	39

Territory	40
Want(ed)	41
Dance Of Grief	42
Letters In April	43
Thunder Lizard	44
Note To Self (Help)	45
Private Thoughts	46
September	47
Concession	48
Lowlands	50
Song	51

Special thanks to J.L. and J.F.

Wildfire

This is the map of the forest fire
This is a drawing of your house
This is a photograph of an enormous
Cloud of smoke
This is a mandatory evacuation
Tomorrow none of this will exist
This is the number of acres
This is the number of the percentage
Of containment. Far smaller
This is the mugshot of the arsonist
This is the orchard, the trees
The grass, the meadow where
The horses were, ablaze all
This is what you remember
This is the beginning
Finally burning down.

True Spring

In this period of rupture
Let sleeping people lie
Allow the childless to rest
Illuminate the past

Here is the place I tell you
I did not ask for it, none of us did

The grapes are ripening. It is spring
The walls are made of question marks
Gone are the days when you thought
You must please everyone, quietly

You are released from all
Imaginary contracts

Here are a fistful of nights that will
Follow you for decades

Stop   [carry them]   Stop

Here are bright, blinding mornings
Of sheer terror

Try [forget them]   Try

Mornings bring memories of night
But I fixed that. I fuzzed the dark
So fogged I couldn't see behind me

I won [I waned] I won

No memories, a sad success
I heard the scrape of shovels

The wisteria in full bloom
Rips the porch from the house
She sleeps under snow
Ravens claw the sky

It is spring again. Time
To wave bright flags, to
Flood the past with light
To finally sift the ruins

Day

The morning has meat on its bones
What is your first thought?
What color is today?
Pale, but stirring
Distant sirens, distant drums
Eyes articulate patterns, colors
Gray-blue, whitecap, sand, and rust
Cylinder, triangle, dune

Over the course of two years
Everyone's fathers died
Nobody told me about mine but
That didn't make him any less dead
Or me any more abandoned.

The morning is minute
I could shatter, a tiny explosion
In this void, but I don't
I see branches, breathe water
I am a drum, or merely a heartbeat
Muffled by fog.

The morning is double-barreled,
Trouble-cluttered, and all-too-familiar
I break into a run and when I do
My hair is blown against my face
Salty, more tendril than tress.

The morning is geometric
There is a right triangle of pure light
On a maroon wall
A rectangle can hold the abstract elk
A feather hints at pre-history

The geode is intact, today
Maybe I will break it open
I'll shuffle out into the light
Hammer in hand. Maybe I'll find
The right tool for the job today
So far, there haven't been any days
When I even cared to look.

Rainbow Trout

My tender feet on gravel pick a path
Alongside the high-stepping goat
Through red rock and dust
To an end-of-summer, slime-hued pond

> (Bullfrogs sleeping deep in mud, conversing
> in the cool of night— their songs ancient, melodic.
> Cannibals, all)

Each time my soles get tougher,
The jab of gravel less severe. Cautious
June gives way to callous August. I move
Swift through July, devouring heat.

> (Turtles snapping, dragonflies fucking
> midair. Empty eyes just above water)

I used to dream of fish— strong, speckled trout,
The lake pollen-dusted in late afternoon sun,
Rippling with minnow and fly.

> (Why did no one teach me? Why didn't anyone
> show me what to do? I had no idea that when the
> blood came so, too, would the sharks)

A Complicated System

Decade on decade stacked
Not leaning or teetering
A fact-solid structure
No, the ghosting was good
Injustice can be illuminating
Your disappearance not the problem
But, rather, a solution
Your absence, a blessing
A lack of violence, or necessity
To build more rooms
In a structure that is already
A complicated system
Walls and valves, sparks flying
People are always starting sentences with,
"What kind of monster would..."
I tune out there
All kinds of monsters
Do all kinds of things

Portuguese Sweet Bread

You taught me how to bake bread, Portuguese sweet bread,
Milk, honey, sugar, yeast, flour, eggs.

Pot-bellied, eyeliner smeared, you, hawked-eyed,
Caught in a moment of kindness.

You said at night a woman can shape shift,
You told me of the many dimensions and showed me your prism.

I inherited your dark eyes and sharp tongue,
Though you never showed me how to use them.

You told me how to speak to the dead and how,
Once invoked, they will do your bidding.

But you didn't teach me restraint, or how to use
My powers for good. You sent me out into the world,

With nothing but weapons.

How The Devil Does

The monster has dirty fingernails
The monster has dead eyes
The monster is male
The monster is handsome at first
But then becomes grotesque
Like how they say the devil does
The monster breathes heavily
And has wet, shiny lips
The monster is someone you know
Not a stranger hiding in the shadows
The monster lives in your house
And slowly turns you
Into a monster, too
I swallow the monster in me
But I can't kill it completely
I try to drown it but it rises
From the tenebrous waters
I am the snake, the cannibal
The bird of prey
I am the new monster
Who, once made,
Kills its creator

Ready Or Not

Buried under organs and tissue
    Blood and miles of veins

    Wherever it is, I am always hidden

Hidden in plain sight
Hidden in small spaces
Hidden in front of a crowd

    (inside out, lost completely)

I wish I had learned how to converse
    When I was fresh-faced and peach-lipped

    When so little was known

I hide in the tall, gossiping grass and
    In dried-up ponds beneath lilac and reed

I disrobe, peel back my skin
    Hang up lung and heart, muscle and tongue

    I strip to blank white bone

There is a lost child hidden under my ribs
    Open the cage and—

    Out she flies.

Signs Say Love, Love More

let our hearts rave on   rave more
burn the buildings   collapse the walls
cancel every language   read only
eyes and gestures   bodies and hands
call down the storms   wrap
    ourselves in radiant light

But I say no.

i'm tired   there's dirt on the floor
i'm hungry   pain and longing   have
whittled me so thin   i am   almost nothing
i have wanted   with the force of oceans

The dams did not break.

i have been soft   so soft i was slippery
i slid a thousand sweet words   into your ears
i unwrapped   every weakness
    laid them naked in your palm

Half Mine

Good morning autumn colors
Good morning evergreen

Hello peach blossom
Hello abalone eyes

Good morning winter melody
Hello delicate spoon

Good morning dark eyes
Good morning soft lips

Hello fire opal
Hello china doll

Hello bright prism
Hello umbrella

Have a good night gumdrop
You too calligraphy brush

Good day colorful balloons
Hello hidden fern

Goodnight flute
Sweet dreams tall ship

Good morning sunlit cypress
Good afternoon scent of leaf

Goodnight sweet kiwi
Goodnight lightning

Good Sunday quilted flower
Hello iridescent feather

Good morning space and time
Good morning jade and pearl

Hello 100 proof
Good evening crystal chandelier

Wading The Shallows

I imagine you again   the weight of you
Your shadowy curls   behind your ears
Feminine tresses   for such a dark man
I think of you   lifting my hips

      Over your mouth

You're a good idea   when I'm lonely
I dream of you   in pineapple rain
While flamingoes   wade the shallows
Without looking up   I know you're there

      Last and any night

Floorboards shiver   the robots hide
We scribble out   some small talk
There's a secret   singe the pages
See the scratches   come while morning

      Burns through the sugared froth

The World Awakes

Long, invisible cords stretch between us
Sometimes they slip through the ropes
That connect other beings
Sometimes they catch, or tangle, or
Caress and become complex knots

Our movements cause vibrations
(The mechanics of our brains, the heat of our bodies)
This is how we communicate
This is why we cannot lie to each other

There are many ways we fit, I notice new ones all the time
When you rest your head on my foot
Your high cheekbone ess-shapes along my ankle
I image cartilage and tendon talking

The wind shakes the tambourine
The prism flings light
The heat speaks a newborn language

I feel the invisible strings begin to hum
They arpeggiate sentiments we never say
Like a hand on a shoulder, they reassure

The world awakes

The Universal Word Is *huh*

Here darkness climbs the tree trunks.
It seeps out of the earth and drips from the sky.
There are meteors that neither of us can see.
Out in the middle of an enormous field
Shivering in twilight, we can say to each other
Things that want to be said.

I can say, Too bad I didn't find you sooner.
You can reply, I wish there was some way.
Then trail off because we can never
Say everything that wants to be said.

You with eyes like seashells, iridescent
Dark and flickering in the coming night.
Your bright voice dances in the rafters.
Tie yourself to me. No one will drown.

Don't forget the war. The good war.
I'm told this and I know what it means.
Go on. Forget me. There are so many
Of me. I am lost in the paperwork.
(Leaves of letters like hands,
Soft then hard in places.)

The sound of your call— a bell banging,
A chime chiming. Blood on the floor.
All free to walk in and witness the scene.
(Gather me up in your gentleness.)
Startle me awake with pure love.
You are kinder than I expected you to be.

After me, go on. Come back and
Show me pictures of your children.
(That feeling of being someone else
entirely without having changed at all.)

But first,

Let's tie ourselves together.
Not to keep from drowning
But because we are made buoyant
By the sight of each other.

Evening

In the evening loneliness like a colorless,
Odorless gas seeps into the room
Immobilizing, it arrests action to a single ache

I go to bed early and sleep late to hide
My inadequacies, my lack of ambition
Or just to take the day off from failure

Frustration is a tall man in a dollhouse
Fumbling the fragile things

I wake thinking that I can hear the vacuum
We are in. I remember your beard whiskers
Brushing my face, rough like a street sweeper
How even in the sheet tangle with sweat-tart skin
It was always a backwards hope

We were always marching toward the beginning
Holding hands once, maybe twice, along the way

Fainter hum of vacuum, fainter thud of heart
Humid air, as if the sun drank all the rain
I stretch my legs long until toes touch your memory
Over the arched spine of time and into those
Gentle days. Not caring that our love was only
A television flicker on an unfamiliar wall

The morning comes threadbare and I remember
How you spoke in cursive, with an italic tongue

Night Creatures

We are birds in the wild
Quick-eyed, hollow-boned
I taste you on the air
I glance at you
You preen your feathers
I pay attention, peripherally
You strut like a cock
Once timid, now hot
You peck my neck
You scratch my flesh
Your beak is wet
Puffed and ruffled we call
Across the tall grass
Through cat tail
And pussy willow
In the chaos of sunset
We recognize each other's songs
In darkness we roost
High in the trees and
Let the night creatures
Take over

Blind Games

At night we play a game where we pretend we are blind
We sit very close so we can reach each other's faces
I touch your forehead, your lips, your ears and neck
I rest my cheek against yours and feel the curve of our bones
Rise and dip against each other, up and down like respiration
Shallow breath, anticipating the knowledge that our separate
Pieces fit and are, once locked together, impossible to take apart.

Let's play a game where you love me like I love you
In this game you are not on your way over to tell me
You won't be coming back and we are not in the middle
Of a heat wave. We haven't angered the Gods. We won't
Stand in the fiery beams, bleeding. We will not burn.
In this game I know the taste of your mouth and your
Skin smells not like your sweat, but mine.

Perfect Geometry

Don't apologize when, mid-gesture, your hand grazes my ass.
I was the one who backed up to get within reach.

You are perfect geometry. I add point of eyelid to angle of bone,
To the tang when you tense, to the line I draw down, down, down—

From soft of mouth to jut of hip.

I want to turn you like a jewel in the light, flip you like a coin.
You always knew how to fuck away a hangover. Come here.

When we come together I transform. You, the invariant one,
Are not my property. What if I burst into flames?

You say, That's the goal of this experiment.

I am windswept, beveled. Your angles are unchanged.
You refract light, your surface clean.

I think of water at night. Below, all of those distant lights.
We slid in, in, in— I lost a silver ring and a drop of blood.

I think of tall trees, how their crowns caress the sky,
Who, blue, slips down around them, through every limb.

And sinking all the way to the ground connects where
Root presses stone, where light douses earth.

Don't apologize when your lips brush my neck. You don't
Hear the ocean saying sorry for lapping up the shore.

Sex & Love Anonymous

Bite-bruised, I walk outside.

Above me power lines crackle with static,
or else it's birds in the trees.
    But it's not birds.
I see when I look lower they are gliding at head height
down the middle of the street in long, sinister single file.

Broken glass, what looks like
a year's worth of crusty diamonds,
litters the street along the children's park.
It's weekly street cleaning here
and the week's not even over yet.

I wonder how many bashed-in windows
it takes to bedazzle a block.

The security guard drowses in the blue-bellied dusk,
Ford Taurus parked on the sidewalk, idling.
I go around, crunching on asphalt and glass.

No one is watching.

A film of dampness sticks to everything,
    not raining, not not raining.
Maddening weather with a hint of tornado
echoing in from the east, clouds too heavy to hover.

Cars are abnormal colors, bright yellow, sickly green.
It's insensitive. Animals pant even at this low temperature.

I go home to find your hat between my bed and the wall.
    Now then, I think,
returning to the scene of the crime
and fluffing a pillow behind my head,
    where was I?

I Change Only The Names Of The Living

_____ has dirty blonde
hair and blue eyes
_____ kisses too hard
uses too much tongue
and bites
_____ is light
where I am dark
I kiss too soft and
touch too often
_____ wants to return
To left-off things
I will drive for miles
rather than backtrack
_____ will say
anything to get free
In that way
_____ and I
are just alike

False Spring

The jasmine blooms in January.
Schizophrenics wake up screaming,
Hurry away the night!
The backyard is a mosquito farm.
I squint and realize I am lonely.
When that happened, I do not know.

All of my dreams are desert dreams now.
There are naked women in single- and
Double-wides, shaved and lacquered.
There are beautiful specimens of flesh and bone
Milling about everywhere, the weather is sultry.

Today is an ocean day,
There is water in the air.
Today is an alligator day,
Belching decomposed hours.
Today is a lion sleeping in the sun,
The pace is glacial.

I live in continual darkness, though.
No one sees it. I can't reach the sun
Or feel its warmth.

Hymn

Feed me gospel in the morning
Poems in the afternoon
And every night, music

    (I am the mayor of this ghost town)

Remind me to open the book
Of animals seeing that man on
His walks, and of why I wanted it

    (I am a peddler of mirrors)

Tell me the coffee is ready
The dog is fed, that you did the dishes
And the cupboards are full

    (I am nobody's wife)

Touch first my burned shoulder, then
Finger the scar on my inner ankle
Throw out the mail, no letters came today

    (I am a tender of gardens)

Teach me to hum underwater
And how to read time signatures
Show me the way to cross a river
One rock at a time

    (My heart is invisible and cannot be ambushed)

Memories Meet Memories

She said, "She lives here," pressing a warm palm into my left side, "beneath your ribs, under your heart." I try to make my breathing rhythmic.

"You carry her with you even though you don't know it. When you are lying down feel for her with your hands, massage and comfort her, acknowledge her presence." I begin to cry without sound.

"Someday you will be able to save her. You will open the cupboard and help her escape. You will pick her up in your arms and carry her out of the door, down the stairs, and into the night. She will be safe and you will be free. At this time she will dissolve and incorporate herself back into your body. You will be whole. You will no longer feel her beneath your ribs, under your heart. You will have saved yourself."

I don't believe her but it is so nice that she has laid her hand on me that I let myself cry for her touch, her gentle voice, for the air around us, and the semi-darkness of the room. Memories meet memories and hover above the place on my body where her palm rests.

Pastels

When I was so young
You were already so old
I was shy and a little afraid
Of the strange odor in your house
But I liked you so the smell
Disappeared as soon as you spoke

You had your lunch delivered
By Meals On Wheels and
The walls in your apartment
Were all painted different colors
Lime sherbet green, Pepto-Bismal pink,
Lilac lavender, and one more color
I can't recall, Aqua Velva blue, maybe

I found this all interesting and
Mysterious. No one had told me yet
That we were poor. You and I
Both knew the lady next door
Was a shape-shifting witch
With dozens of familiars prowling
You never pretended she wasn't

The first time I remember
Knowing what had happened
Before anyone told me
Was the night the phone rang late
When I was so young
And you were already so old

Bright Ribbons

Sirens through the days
and nights— louder in the heat
with every window open—
but barely noticed now

We keep the fan on
to soften the sounds— there are
small birds twittering in the
purple-flowered tree— we
listen closely to their chirps

The hummingbirds make
light, elegant noises to match
their light, elegant bodies—
I imagine I hear their
wings beating

I want to listen to birdsong
unfurling like bright ribbons
through the branches
and squawk with you
from some restful perch

Two

Days gone beside the river
sweet peas in the water
home, and back
to hard wind and strong drink
eyes of questions
a sigh on cracked lips
working the long shift
   early 'til late
hungry and dreaming
robbed twice in the ruins.

(A maze of water,
an urn of steam,
corridor of pools— afraid
at first, to get wet—
floating platforms
at varied distances.)

Nothing uniform—
all surrounded by water
I can't see through.
Messages when I wake
on the manmade shore,
indoors. Farewells, good-byes,
a pageful of until-laters.

(Is it closer to the door
at the end of the maze
or to go back and leave
the way I came in?)

Outside all the injured and dead
get up and run.

Location

Sometimes I think about architecture.
I think of building. I construct a room.
I add to it. It holds me and all the things
I think I need. I imagine myself living inside it.
I grow attached to it, never want to leave.
It is made of wood, stone, and glass.
It is cool and quiet and close to a body
of water, a river, or channel.

This is a meditation.

When I go out walking I look into windows.
I wonder about the people who live in the places I pass.
I wonder what they worry over, if they are alright.
I have told you that before.
I have told you everything I have ever told you
twice at least. I am embarrassed by how much I repeat myself.

Stop me if you've heard this!

When I was a baby I slept in a drawer.
When I was a child I hid in the cupboard
waiting for things to go quiet.
When I was young I ran outside.
I searched a thousand rooms. I never felt safe.
Walls can be shaken. Doors can lock you in.
It is always an earthquake. It's safer out in the open.
Head to high ground and I'll meet you there.

Brothers

They chased you like a pack of hornets.
I, laughing, locked the door.
Cruel children, we both. Violent.
I didn't know they were stinging your flesh.

Or maybe I did. I didn't say goodbye.
We lived too far in the shadows
To use words like that.

I have to be the fire tearing across the field
Drunk on light. Burning everything behind me.

Olivine. Birthstone. Bad genes. Birthright.
Addictive, grasping, hoping humans. Both.
Gentle now, and beaten by time.

You don't have to carry the coffin.
We buried it years ago and I slept
On the grave. I'll be something for us both.

You, the family man.
Me, the wayward son.

Without you the three points are broken.
Come back from the deep ocean, silver fish.
I can hear the call through the water.

You, the shadowed mountains.
Me, the frozen sky.
We retreated to our cold places. I know.

Me, Not A Mother

Tomorrow I will teach you to make coffee
Tomorrow the heat, the steam, the clink of spoon
on cup edge and saucer

There will be cream and honey and the room
will fill with that exotic aroma—
we will share the ritual— talk of daytime things
in the kitchen, the heart of the house

I will tell you they are out there
trying to find him and I will wonder
why I am not. As time and options run
out, we hope he comes home

I will tell you but never her
that I don't think it will work—
(why would it now?)

While I'm teaching you to make coffee,
you won't know it but, by listening to me
you will have saved a mother grief

You, a mother, her, a mother, me, not a mother
And it's true what they say, unless you are
you can't understand

Sonogram

The first thing I thought of when I saw my heart was a rabbit, scared and running. It was beating so fast. How was it able to keep going at that rate? I suddenly wanted very much to go to sleep. It was hard to believe I was looking inside my own body, peering at this hunk of meat that housed all of my love, my hate, my pain. I looked for scars, for visible cracks where it had been broken, for bruises. It looked foreign, black and white, throbbing, desperately pressed in there against— I don't know what it was pressed against. I was curious why it hadn't grown huge with all that pounding, this muscle in my chest.

I think about it sometimes, but not very much. It makes me feel scared, like I saw something I shouldn't have. It makes me feel remote and lonely, then guilty because it's a part of me. It works hard to keep me alive. I should love it more. I shouldn't be afraid of this wild thing thrashing inside me, but I am. I haven't seen it since then and it was a long time ago. I know it has a scar from where they burned it with electricity. There are probably cracks now, too, and other signs of wear.

Territory

You're out where
Moon and sun, like scales
Hang on opposite horizons

Your being the bridge
Between them, amid
A million lakes

I have space finally
All, in fact, of the
Lower forty-eight

You are north, where
The Yukon pools around
Your naked ankles

You eavesdrop on
Moose and evergreen
Twilight falls beside the
Backward swimming fish

Want(ed)

I want to show you the cool underside of a leaf,
Or shine on you warm lights that won't burn out.

I want to hand you an armful of emerald fronds,
And wash the dust from your well-traveled feet.

No two cricket legs sing the same song.
(There are days when I miss you and pretend
We were so much happier than we really were.)
I rub my limbs and search the sheets.

I wanted to give away everything I made—
To sweep all the time capsules from space.

Here, take these, I said. Now they are yours.
I lifted, lightened from the weight of those days,
And ran forward, heart racing and bumping,
Like an old truck down a rutted road.

Dance Of Grief

I see you and am tossed back
To the brief time I carried you
Close, in the palm of my hand

All the trying is erased
I want to pull you to me
To take you home, or
For us to be deserters, again

I want to care for you but also,
Tear you apart piece by piece
I come home, to bed, still starving
Wind-battered on a lonely shore

The next day summer arrives suddenly
In all its knobby-kneed glory, guileless
Caressed, I open and you slip free, again

Letters In April

I wrote letters in April, poems in September
Your whereabouts unknown

In the early hours of this morning
I gave you my wages and wished you well

Boys, bright-eyed and wary, watch me
The night is caramel, the morning is ash

Beneath the wind-beaten cypress
In view of the huge, obscene cross, kneel down

Throw out the cracked shadow, the torn rug
And dry pen. All that is empty, leave.

Thunder Lizard

In the apocalypse we'll meet on Bernal Hill,
I say it casually. You nod, half-turn, smile, wave bye.
High ground, I say, but you are already gone.

The earthquake kit has yet to arrive but I have
Extra cans of dog food and every intention of
Buying several gallons of water.

We became adults when we weren't looking.
I support National Public Radio and
Chose the earthquake kit as my free gift.

Fun fact:
Brontosaurus means thunder lizard.
I text message you this and we agree
It is useful information.

We discuss what we will eat and when we
Each have to go to work tonight.
I've decided to stay in bed all day, you say.
I tell you that has been my plan all along.

This, our afternoon ritual. The midday check-in.
See you in the hellmouth, I say,
Either that or on the hill.

Note To Self (Help)

Remember to remember,
Hard liquor gives you heartburn.

Remember to remember,
Scary movies don't give you bad dreams, but they make you unable to sleep on a random night, sometimes weeks or months later.

Remember to remember,
Relax the muscles in your face when being photographed. You look jowly and grumpy and your features get even more crooked than usual when you don't.

Remember to mail the check by the 23rd, pay the phone bill by the 10th, and that there is a birthday party on Sunday.

Remember to remember,
Just because you fucked up yet again, it doesn't mean you never did anything right.

Private Thoughts

Inside my mind
When I'm alone
When no one is listening
And nobody's home

    I'm a really good...
        dancer.

When I'm alone
Inside my mind
There's a big empty room
With just you and I

    And we are...
        dancing.

September

This isn't a summer morning,

I am no longer in my thirties,

and both of my parents are not alive.

The young man who smiled

so sweetly in the springtime is gone.

It is just me and the creeping light,

the yawning dog and the ashes,

the flowers silently shedding petals

on the floor.

Concession

It was a really bad year
A confusion of swirling seasons

Winter followed Spring
Summer came too late
Then tried to make up for it
With unrelenting fire

The crooks won the prizes
All the wrong people died
I winced beneath the bright tower
I wanted out of debt

We lost our homes, our hope
Disillusion abounded
In that oppressive heat
Darkness surrounded us

I struggled against the murk
Half my life passed in one long
    whooooooooosh——
Lost in translation, child to woman

So much has changed
Nothing has changed

I have no idea what season
Will be coming next
Or how we can possibly
Weather more storms.

Lowlands

Raise me above sea level
I need harsh light and fresh water
A glacial lake, stones rough
Sky sage-singed, and a bath of lightning

Listen, there is no clarity here
And it's damp
Drunkenness and depression—
Tame waves, never-ending

Throw away everything but a drum (dream)
A long black gown, and a lavender flute
Get me to the desert where I can
Feed my heart to the glaring sun

Song

In the now-here-we-are of tonight,
I draw a ring around my feet.
Stand here. Don't move.

You are out there,
Lying in wait. Harmless,
A decorative weapon.

The sun sank. It always does.
Monsters slunk out of the waves.
I, shivering, retreated inland.

Someday there will be no me,
Sing the nightbirds, devouring fish.

Someday there will be no me,
Sings the cold moon, off-key.

www.ingramcontent.com/pod-product-compliance
Lightning Source LLC
Chambersburg PA
CBHW031430290426
44110CB00011B/595